THE NATURE KIDS GUIDE TO
TIGERS

DAVID ANDERSON

LP Media Inc. Publishing
Text copyright © 2026 by LP Media Inc.
All rights reserved.

For information address LP Media Inc. Publishing,
30012 Variolite St NW, Princeton MN 55371
www.lpmedia.org

Publication Data

Tigers
The Nature Kid's Guide to Tigers — First edition.

Summary: "Learn all about Tigers, the Nature Kid Way"
— Provided by publisher.

ISBN: 979-8-89818-094-2

[1. Tigers – Non-Fiction] I. Title.

Title: The Nature Kid's Guide to Tigers

CONTENTS

JUNGLE HOME

DID YOU KNOW?
Tigers once lived across most of Asia. Today, they live in only 13 countries. India has the most wild tigers. More than 3,600 tigers live in India.

Growl! A tiger walks through tall grass. Its stripes help it hide.

Tigers make their homes in many places. Some tigers live in thick jungles. Others live in snowy forests. Tigers need land with trees and bushes.

Tigers stay where they can find water. They drink from rivers and streams. Tigers also swim to cool off, and they are very good at it!

Each tiger needs a lot of space. This space is called its territory. Tigers travel through parts of their territory every day. They know every path and hiding spot.

TIGER TURF

Roar! A tiger stands by a river, guarding its home.

Tigers once roamed across many countries. Now they live in fewer places.

Tigers can be found in India, Russia, and Southeast Asia. Some tigers live where it is hot. Others live where snow falls in winter.

Tigers need large areas with lots of prey. They also need safe places to raise cubs.

A tiger's territory can be up to 770 square miles. That is larger than most cities!

SUPER
SIZED

A tiger pushes through tall grass. Only its head pokes above the top!

Tigers are the biggest wild cats in the world. They are larger than lions, leopards, and jaguars.

Male tigers are bigger than females. A male can weigh up to 660 pounds. That is as heavy as four adult humans!

Tigers can grow over ten feet long from nose to tail. A tiger may eat 88 pounds of meat in one meal.

A tiger's paw is about the size of a dinner plate. Each paw has sharp claws.

STRIPES AND CLAWS

Snap! A tiger stretches its paw, and sharp claws slide out.

Every tiger has stripes. No two tigers have the same pattern. These stripes are like fingerprints, so each tiger looks different from every other tiger.

Tiger fur can be orange, white, or golden. The stripes on this fur are usually black or brown. Stripes cover a tiger's whole body, even its skin!

Tigers also have sharp claws on each paw. The claws can be four inches long. Tigers pull their claws in when they walk. This keeps the claws sharp for catching prey.

A tiger usually has around 100 stripes on its body. Stripes help hide them.

SHARP SENSES

Whoosh! A tiger turns its head. It heard a sound from far away.

Tigers have amazing senses. Their eyes see well in the dark. This helps them hunt at night.

Their ears can also turn in different directions. This lets them hear sounds that humans cannot hear.

Tigers have a strong sense of smell too. They use their nose to track prey and find other tigers nearby.

Tigers can hear sounds from almost two miles away!

HIDDEN HUNTER

Rustle! A tiger crouches low in the grass. Its stripes make it hard to see.

Tigers use their stripes to hide. The stripes break up the shape of their body. This makes them blend in with tall grass and shadows.

Tigers hide to catch prey. They stay still and wait. Their orange and black colors also help them match the forest light.

This hiding trick is called camouflage. It helps tigers sneak up on animals without being seen.

Tigers can sneak within 30 feet of prey before they pounce. Soft paw pads help them walk silently.

MEAT MEALS

Chomp! A tiger bites into its meal and eats fast. It is hungry!

Tigers are carnivores, which means they eat meat. Sometimes they nibble on grass to help their stomachs feel better, but meat is their real food.

Tigers hunt many animals for food. They eat deer, wild pigs, and buffalo. Sometimes they catch fish or birds too.

A tiger can eat up to 88 pounds of meat in one meal. After eating, a tiger may rest for several days.

Tigers need about 15 pounds of meat each day.

SNEAK ATTACK

A tiger can leap forward up to 30 feet in a single jump when attacking its prey.

Pounce! A tiger leaps from the bushes. It catches its prey!

Tigers are sneaky hunters. They do not chase animals for long distances. Instead, they creep close before attacking.

A tiger moves slowly through the grass. It stays low to the ground. When it gets close enough, it jumps forward fast.

Tigers grab prey with their front paws. They use their strong jaws to bite the neck. Most of these hunts happen at night when it is dark.

Tigers only catch prey about one out of every ten tries. This is why they must be patient hunters.

TOP CAT

Snarl! A tiger shows its teeth. This fierce cat is the top predator here.

Tigers are apex predators. This means no other animal hunts them for food. They are at the top of the food chain.

Tigers help keep forests healthy. When they hunt, they control the number of deer and pigs. With fewer plant-eaters, more trees and grass can grow.

Without tigers, the forest would change. Too many plant-eaters would harm the trees and grass.

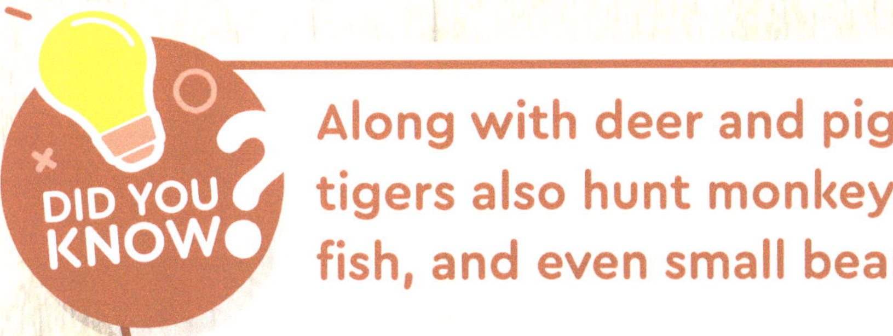

21

STAY SAFE

Splash! A tiger jumps into a river. It swims away from danger.

Adult tigers have few natural enemies, but humans and crocodiles can be dangerous. Tigers can also get hurt in fights with other tigers.

Tigers use water to escape because they are strong swimmers. This helps them cross rivers to reach safety.

Young tigers face more risks. Their mothers protect them until they grow big.

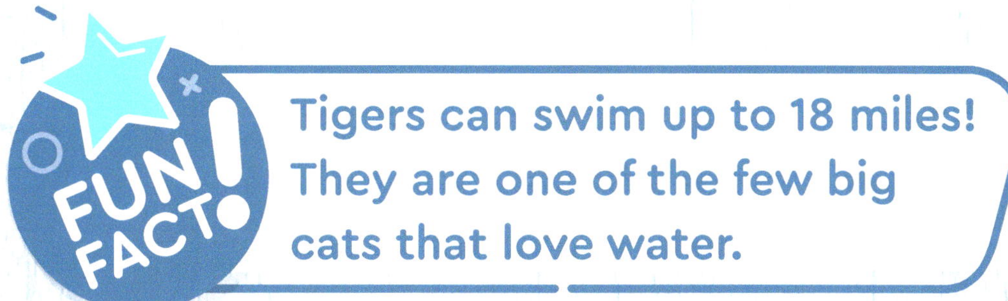

23

FAST FEET

Swoosh! A tiger races through the forest. Its big paws pound the ground.

Tigers are fast runners. They can run up to 40 miles per hour. But they cannot keep this speed for very long.

Their back legs are very strong. Tigers can jump forward about 30 feet in one leap. That's as long as a school bus!

Their speed in short bursts helps them to catch prey.

Tigers can only chase prey for about 100 yards before stopping. They hunt using surprise!

NIGHT PROWL

A tiger moves through the dark forest. Its eyes search for prey.

Tigers are most active at night. They hunt when the sun goes down. This is called being nocturnal.

Darkness helps tigers sneak up on prey. Their eyes see well in low light, so they can spot animals that cannot see them.

Tigers also hunt at dawn and dusk. They rest during the hottest part of the day because cool nights are better for hunting.

Tigers can see six times better in the dark than humans can. This helps them hunt at night.

SOLO
STALKER

Crack! A twig snaps under a tiger's paw as it walks through the forest.

Tigers live alone most of the time. Each tiger has its own territory, unlike lions who live in groups.

Male tigers have larger territories than females. A male's area may overlap with several female territories.

Tigers mark their land with scent. They also scratch trees to leave signs. This tells other tigers to stay away.

Tigers only meet to mate or when mothers raise cubs. Cubs stay with mom for two to three years.

ROARING
ROMANCE

ROAR! A tiger calls out loudly. This sound can travel very far.

When male tigers grow up, they look for a mate.

Tigers use loud calls to find each other. They also leave scent marks. Together, these signals help tigers locate mates across large distances.

Female tigers can have cubs at any time of year. After mating, the male leaves. The female raises the cubs alone.

Male tigers sometimes travel over 600 miles searching for a mate and new territory.

TINY TIGERS

White Bengal tigers are very rare. Only about 1 in every 10,000 tiger cubs is born with white fur!

Purrr! A rare white Bengal tiger cub opens its eyes for the first time.

Tiger cubs are born very small. They weigh only two to three pounds at birth, and their eyes stay closed for about ten days.

Cubs drink their mother's milk at first. Then they start eating meat when they are about two months old. This meaty diet helps them grow fast.

Young tigers stay with their mother for two to three years. During this time, she teaches them how to hunt. Once they learn, they leave to find their own territory.

MOM KNOWS BEST

Grunt! A mother tiger carries her cub gently in her mouth.

Mother tigers are very protective. They keep their cubs hidden in a safe den for the first few weeks.

Moms teach cubs important skills. Cubs watch their mother hunt and learn by copying her. She brings them food until they can catch their own.

A mother tiger moves her cubs to a new den if she senses danger. She carries them one by one to new hiding spots. This keeps them safe from other predators who might find the den.

Cubs learn to recognize their mother's voice within days of birth.

TROUBLE
AHEAD

A tiger stops at the edge of a forest. The trees end here.

Tigers face big problems today. People cut down forests where tigers live. This leaves tigers with fewer places to hunt and raise cubs.

Some people hunt tigers illegally. This is called poaching.

Tigers need large areas to roam. But roads and farms break up forests. This makes it hard for tigers to find each other.

One hundred years ago, about 100,000 wild tigers existed. Today, only around 5,500 remain.

TIGERS
TOMORROW

Click! A camera snaps a photo of a tiger in the wild.

People work hard to save tigers. Many countries protect forests where tigers live. Guards watch over these safe areas.

Some tigers now live in new forests. Scientists move them to places with more space and food.

The number of wild tigers is slowly growing. More tigers live in the wild today than ten years ago.

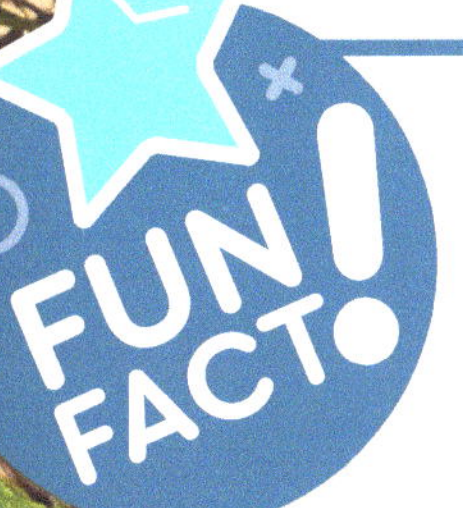

India created the world's first tiger reserve in 1973. Today, India has over 50 reserves.

GLOSSARY

territory

An area of land that an animal lives in and protects as its own.

camouflage

Colors or patterns that help an animal hide by blending in with the things around it.

carnivores

Animals that eat only meat.

apex predators

Animals at the top that no other animals hunt for food.

nocturnal

Active at night instead of during the day.